The Twelve Days of Christmas

◆

◆

ISBN 0-7935-3531-X

© The Walt Disney Company

HAL•LEONARD™
CORPORATION

7777 W. BLUEMOUND RD. P.O. BOX 13819 MILWAUKEE, WI 53213

THE TWELVE DAYS OF CHRISTMAS

Traditional
Arranged by RICHARD FRIEDMAN

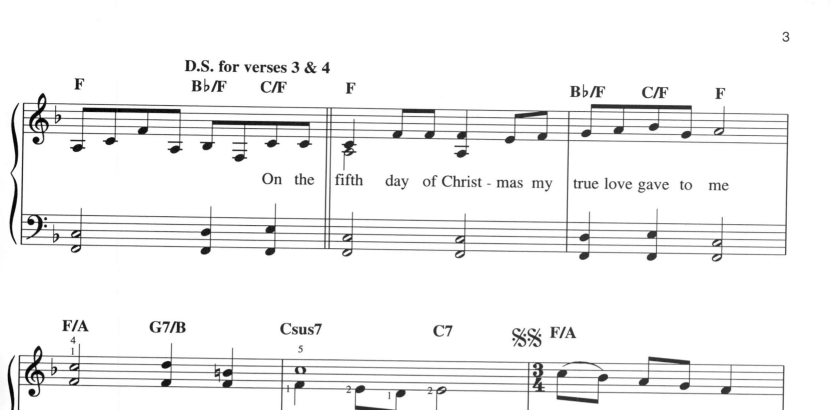

On the fifth day of Christ-mas my true love gave to me
five gold-en rings! _____ Four _ call-ing birds,

three French hens, two _ tur-tle doves, and a par-tridge _ in a pear

last time To Coda

tree.

6. On the sixth day of Christ-mas my true love gave to me
7. On the sev-enth day of Christ-mas my true love gave to me
8. On the eighth day of Christ-mas my true love gave to me
9. On the ninth day of Christ-mas my true love gave to me

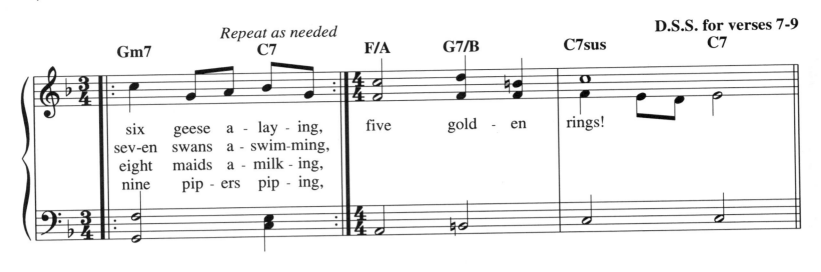

Repeat as needed

D.S.S. for verses 7-9

six geese a - lay - ing, / five gold - en / rings!
sev-en swans a - swim-ming,
eight maids a - milk - ing,
nine pip - ers pip - ing,

CODA

tree.

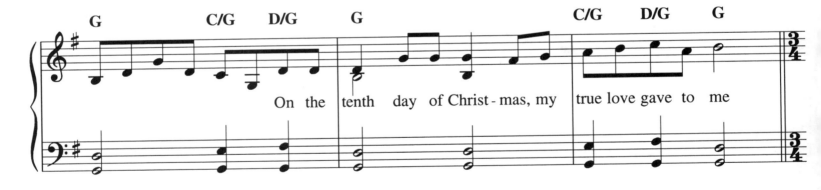

On the tenth day of Christ - mas, my true love gave to me

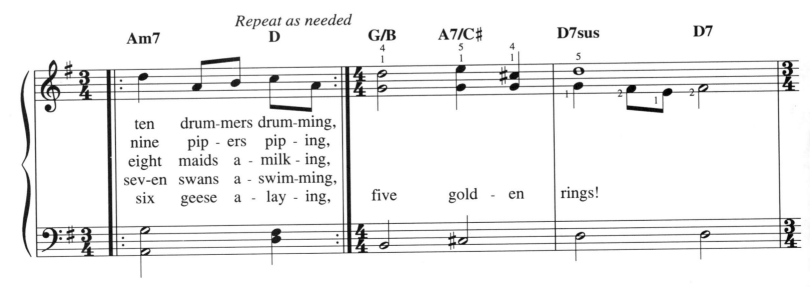

Repeat as needed

ten drum-mers drum-ming, / five gold - en / rings!
nine pip - ers pip - ing,
eight maids a - milk - ing,
sev-en swans a - swim-ming,
six geese a - lay - ing,

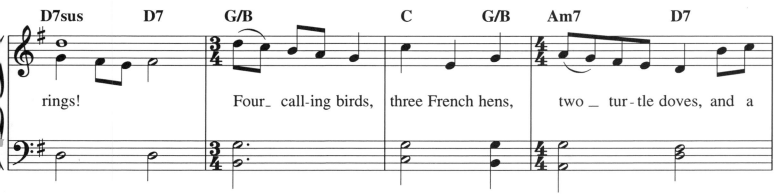

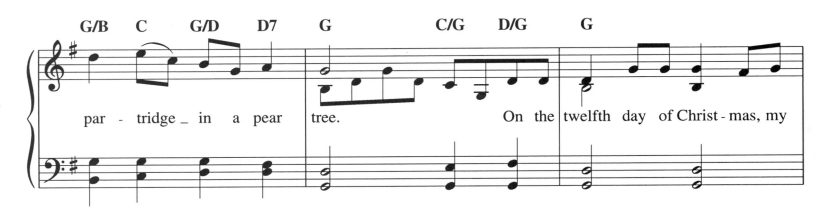

par - tridge _ in a pear tree. On the twelfth day of Christ - mas, my

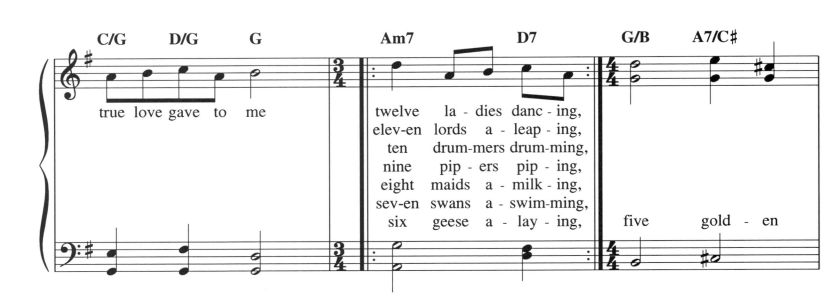

true love gave to me twelve la - dies danc - ing,
elev-en lords a - leap - ing,
ten drum-mers drum-ming,
nine pip - ers pip - ing,
eight maids a - milk - ing,
sev-en swans a - swim-ming,
six geese a - lay - ing, five gold - en

rings! Four_ call-ing birds, three French hens, two _ tur - tle doves, and a

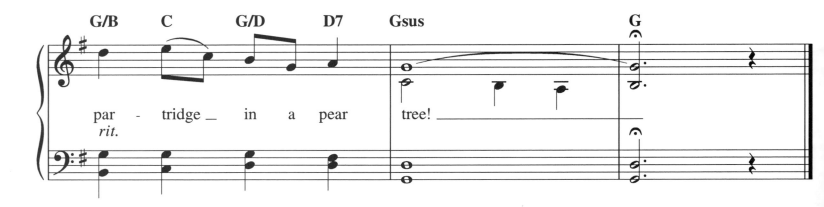

par - tridge _ in a pear tree! _____
rit.

JINGLE BELLS/
SLEIGH RIDE THROUGH THE SNOW

JINGLE BELLS
Traditional
Arranged by RICHARD FRIEDMAN

SLEIGH RIDE THROUGH THE SNOW
Words and Music by ANDY DiTARANTO
and SAMUEL J. WISNER

8

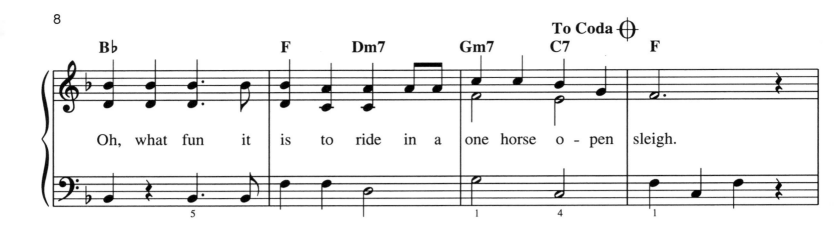

Oh, what fun it is to ride in a one horse o - pen sleigh.

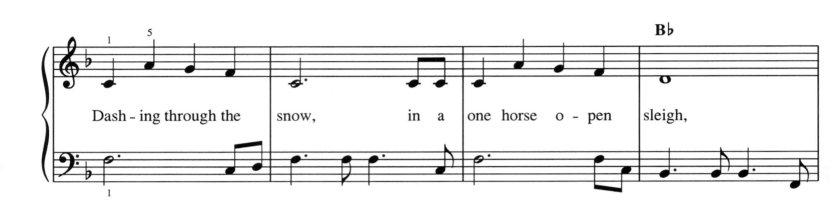

Dash - ing through the snow, in a one horse o - pen sleigh,

o'er the fields we go, laugh - ing all the way.

Bells on bob - tails ring, mak - ing spir - its bright. What

9

SLEIGH RIDE THROUGH THE SNOW

We're glid - ing through the snow in a one horse
So come a - long with us, you'll be de -

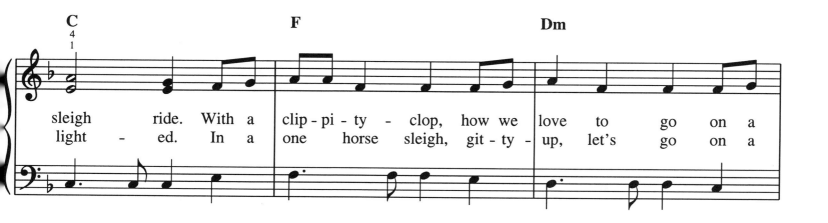

sleigh ride. With a clip - pi - ty - clop, how we love to go on a
light - ed. In a one horse sleigh, git - ty - up, let's go on a

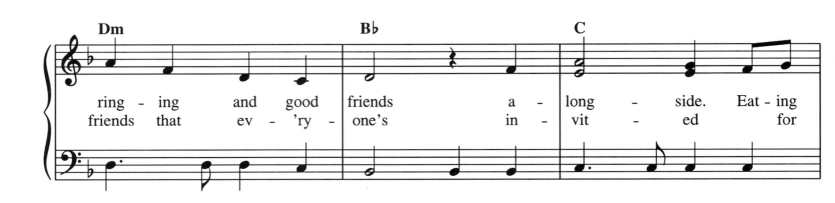

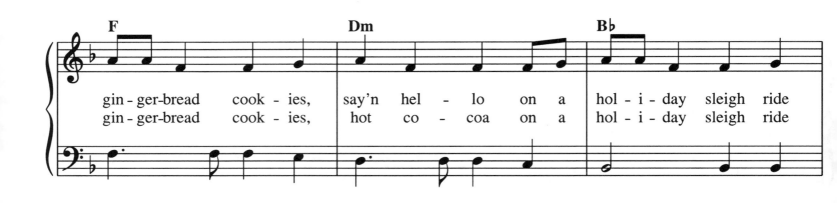

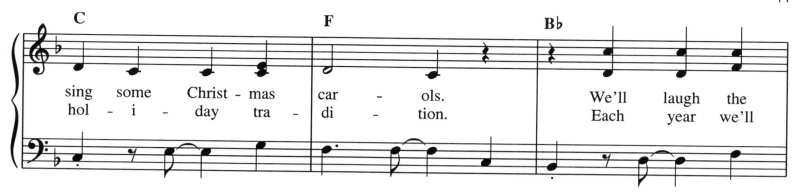

sing some Christ - mas car - ols.
hol - i - day tra - di - tion.
We'll laugh the
Each year we'll

whole day through,
wait for you,
'cause it's the
'cause it's the
sea - son to have
sea - son to have

fun.)
fun.}
Let's go on a sleigh ride through the

snow. For - get your shop-pin' we're jin - gle

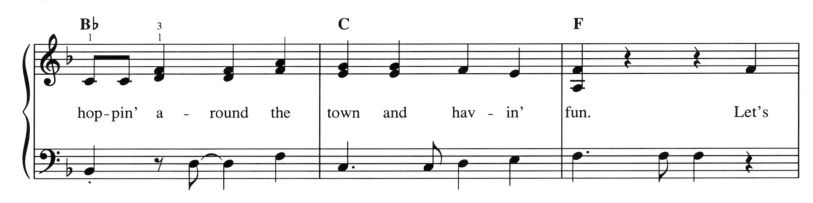

hop-pin' a - round the town and hav - in' fun. Let's

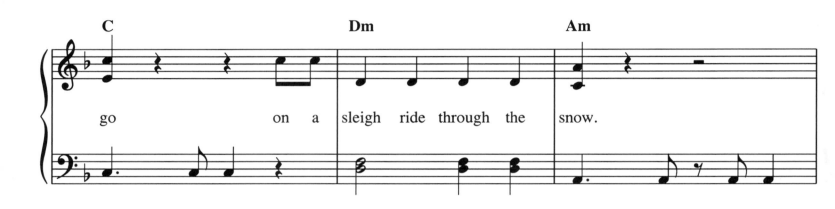

go on a sleigh ride through the snow.

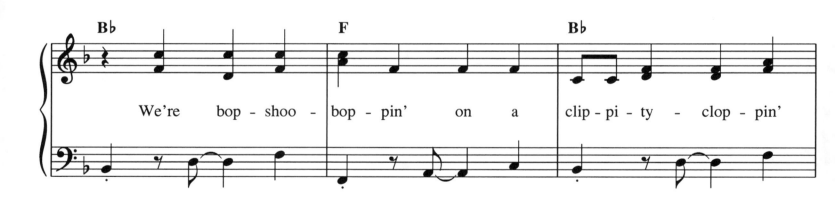

We're bop - shoo - bop-pin' on a clip-pi-ty - clop-pin'

sleigh ride through the snow.

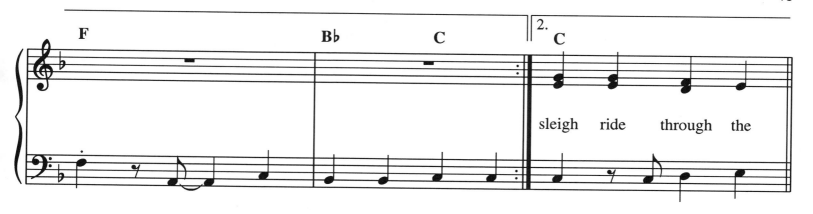

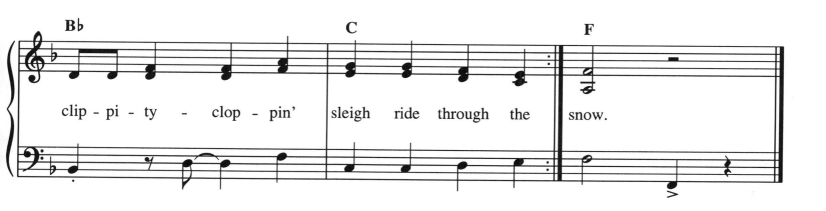

CHRISTMAS TOGETHER/
O CHRISTMAS TREE

CHRISTMAS TOGETHER
Words and Music by
PHIL BARON

O CHRISTMAS TREE
Traditional
Additional lyrics by ROBIN FREDERICK

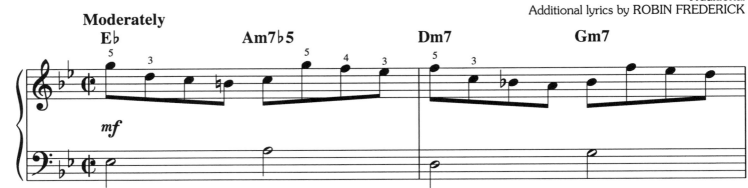

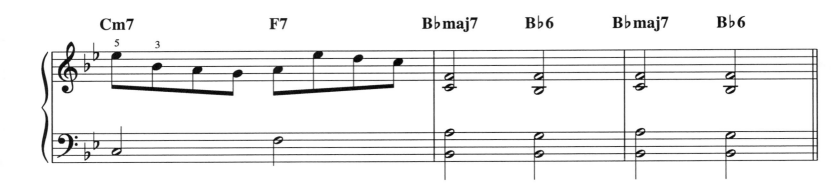

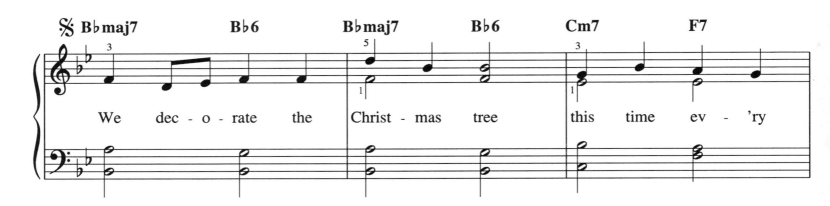

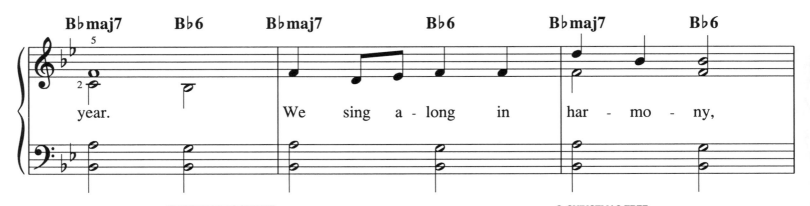

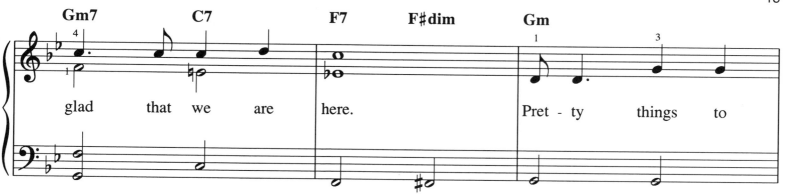

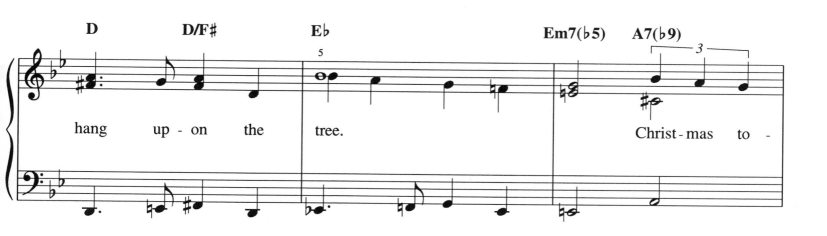

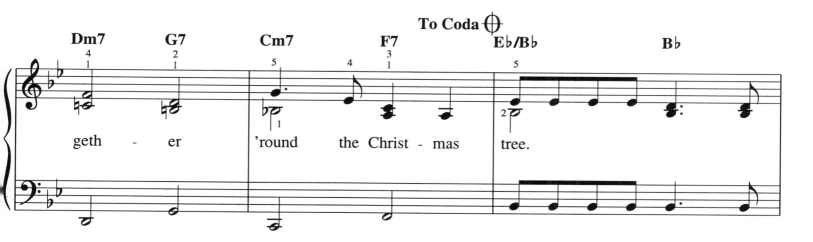

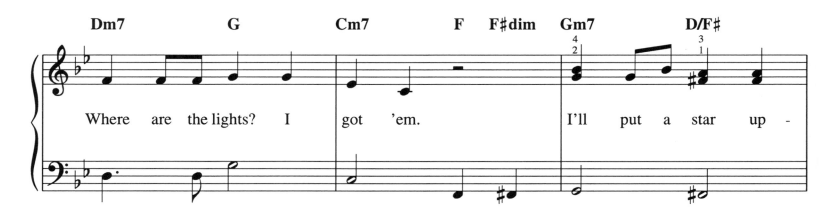

Where are the lights? I got 'em. I'll put a star up -

on the top. And don't for - get the pres - ents

on the bot - tom.

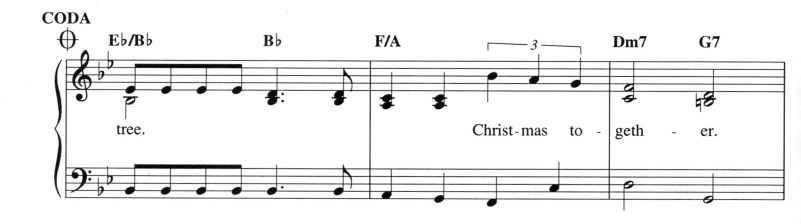

tree. Christ - mas to - geth - er.

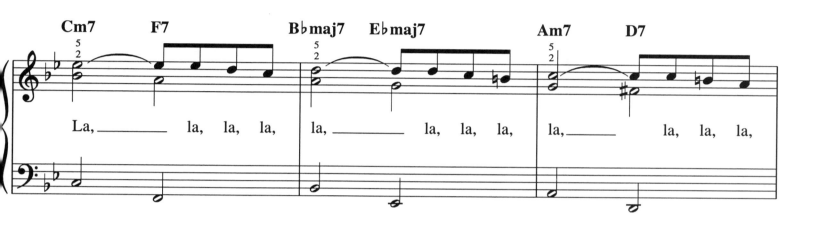

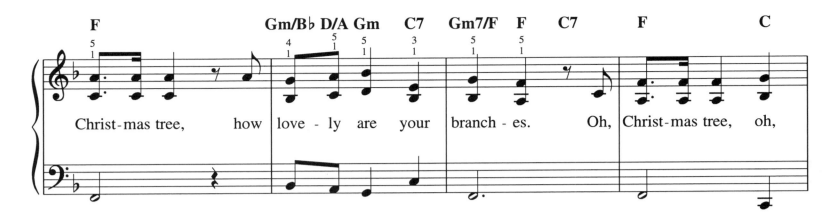

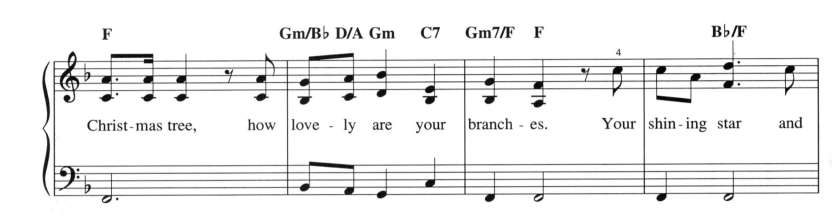

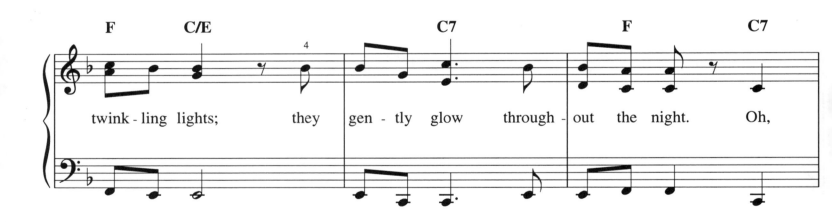

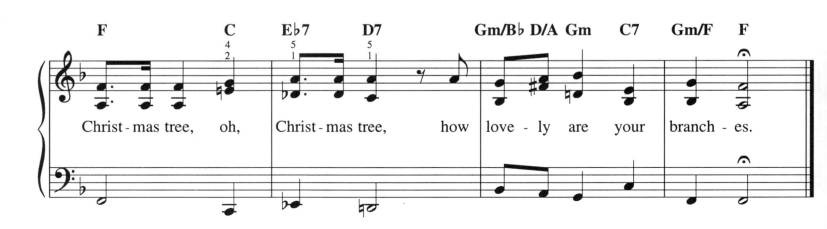

A GIFT OF LOVE

Words and Music by MICHAEL SILVERSHER
and PATTY SILVERSHER

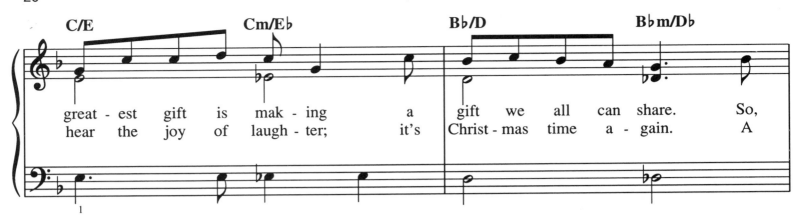

greatest gift is making a gift we all can share. So,
hear the joy of laughter; it's Christmas time again. A

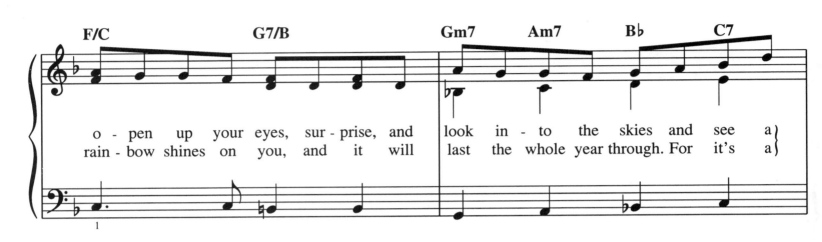

o - pen up your eyes, sur - prise, and look in - to the skies and see a
rain - bow shines on you, and it will last the whole year through. For it's a

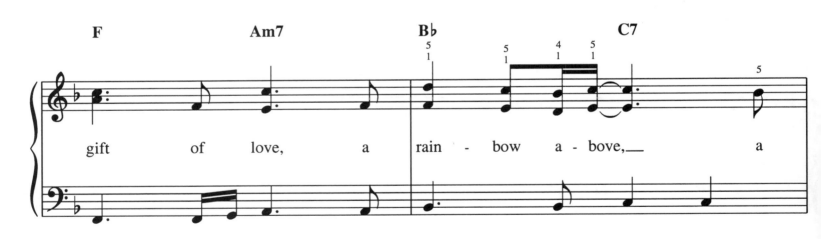

gift of love, a rain - bow a - bove,___ a

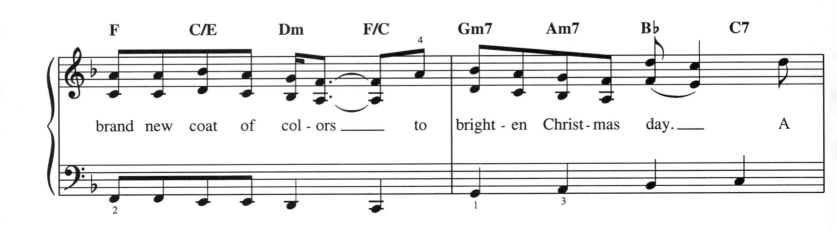

brand new coat of col - ors ___ to bright - en Christ - mas day. ___ A

gift   of love,   filled   with hope   and   light,   a

Christ - mas gift   to   share,   a gift   of   love.

When the   love.

gift of love, a rain - bow a - bove, __ a

brand new coat of col - ors ____ to bright - en Christ - mas day. ____ A

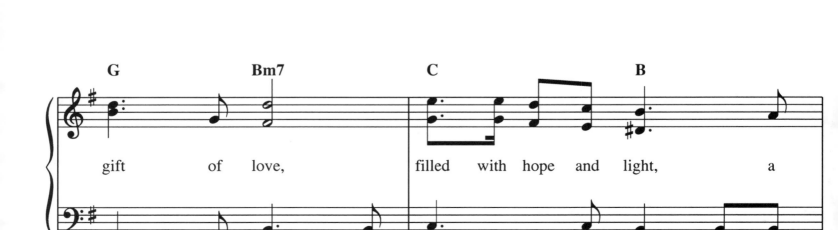

gift of love, filled with hope and light, a

DEAR SANTA

Words and Music by MICHAEL SILVERSHER
and PATTY SILVERSHER

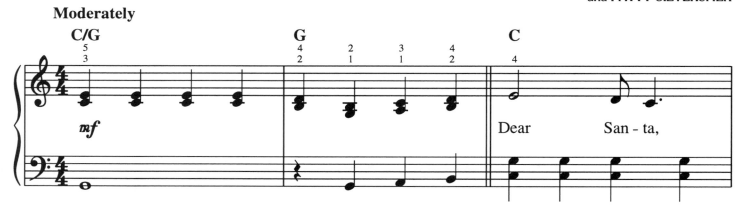

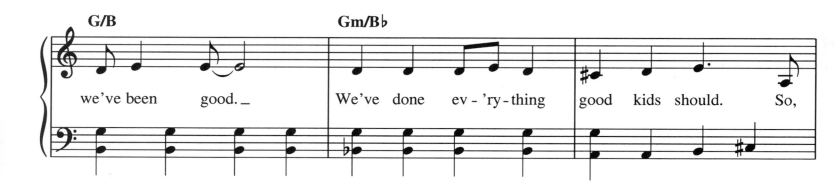

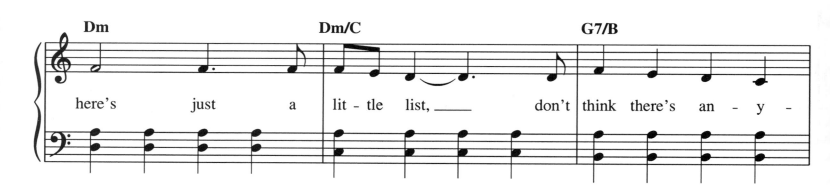

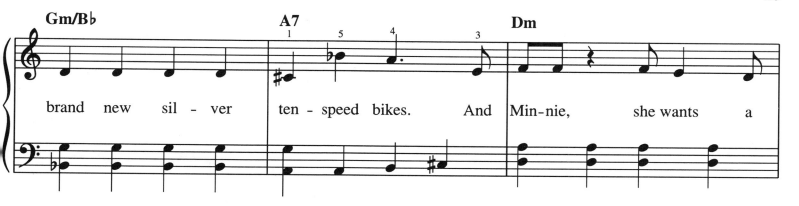

brand new sil - ver ten - speed bikes. And Min - nie, she wants a

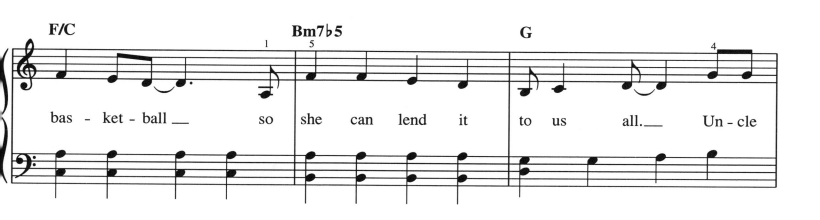

bas - ket - ball __ so she can lend it to us all. __ Un - cle

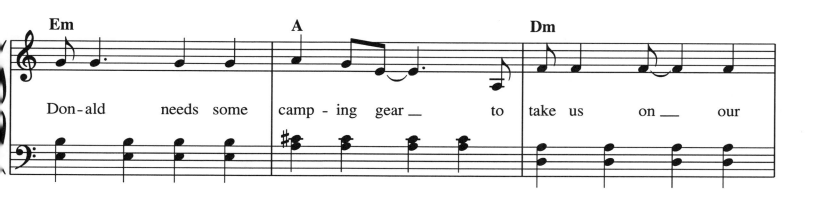

Don - ald needs some camp - ing gear __ to take us on __ our

trip this year. As for us, oops! Well, we al - most for - got.

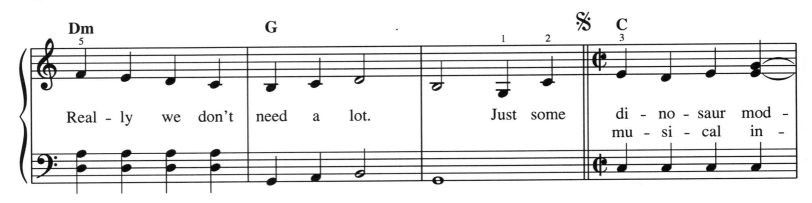

Really we don't need a lot. Just some di - no - saur mod -
mu - si - cal in -

- els, ten vid - e - o games,___ an en - gine and ca -
stru - ment that's eas - y to play,___ a pol - ka - dot um -

boose; be - tween thir - ty - five trains,___ some com - ics,
brel - la for a rain - y day,___ some flow - ers for

rec - ords, and base - ball cards,___ three foot - balls,
Min - nie, red ros - es will do,___ a bone for

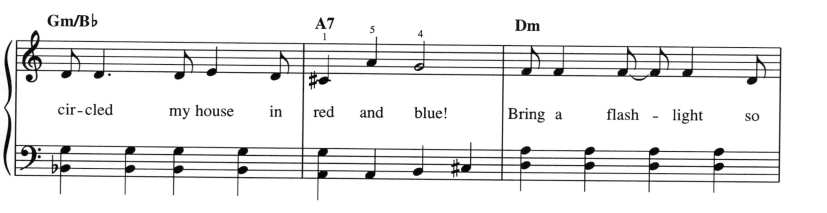

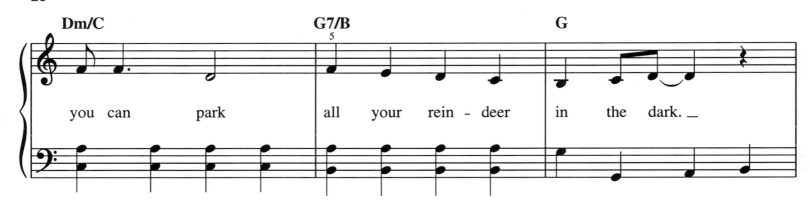

you can park   all   your   rein - deer   in   the   dark. __

Dear   San - ta,   we've   been   so   good. _   We've   done   ev - 'ry-thing

good   folks   should.   I'll   leave   out   milk   and   cook - ies   too. __   Oh,

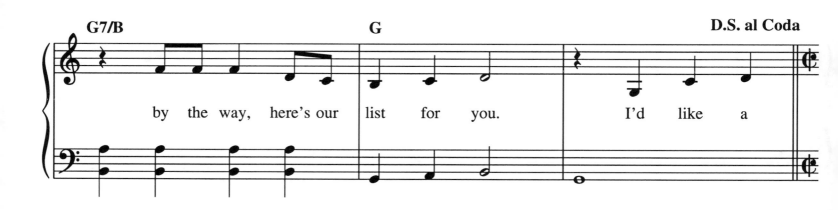

by   the   way,   here's   our   list   for   you.   I'd   like   a

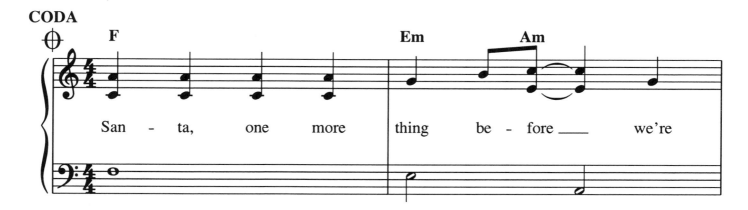

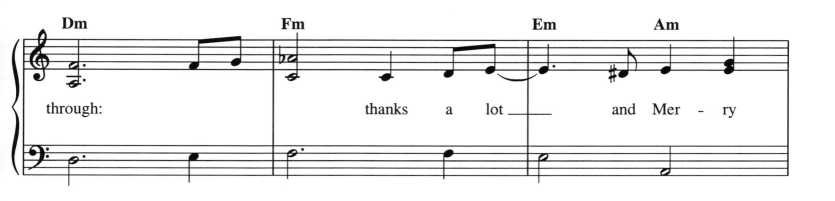

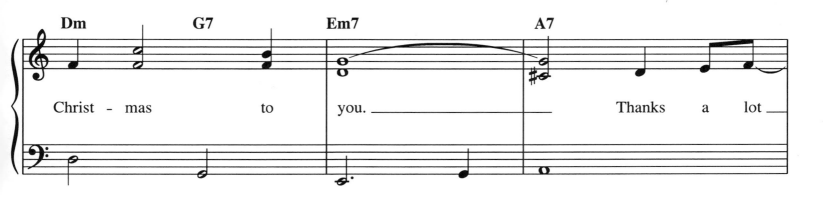

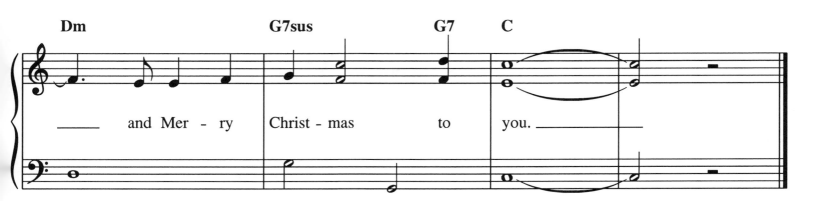

HERE WE COME A-CAROLING/
WE WISH YOU A MERRY CHRISTMAS

Traditional
Arranged by RICHARD FRIEDMAN

Quickly, in one

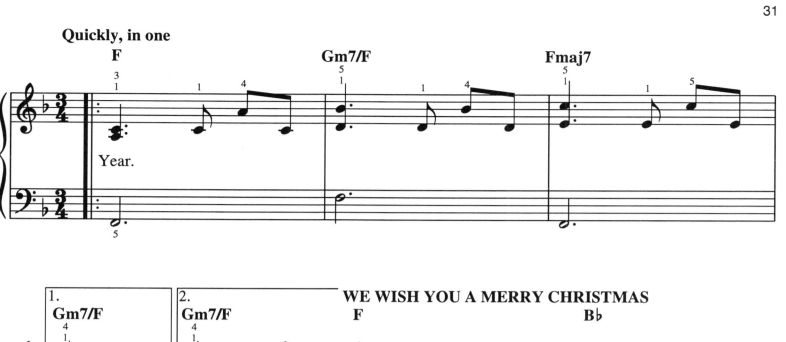

Year.

WE WISH YOU A MERRY CHRISTMAS

We wish you a Mer - ry Christ - mas, we

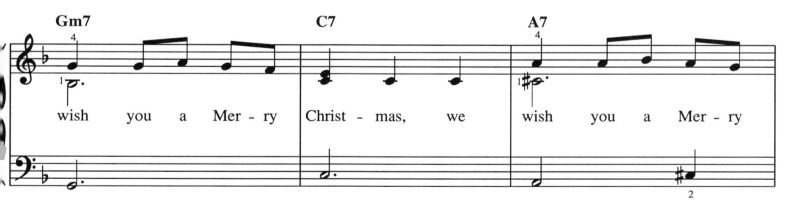

wish you a Mer - ry Christ - mas, we wish you a Mer - ry

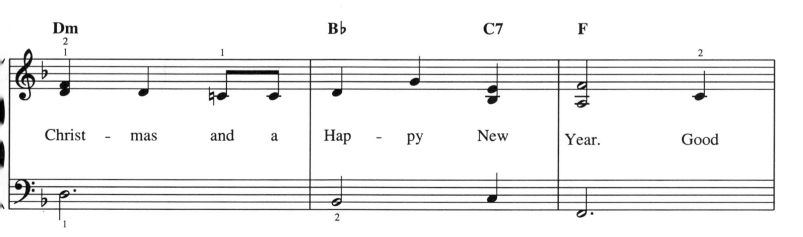

Christ - mas and a Hap - py New Year. Good

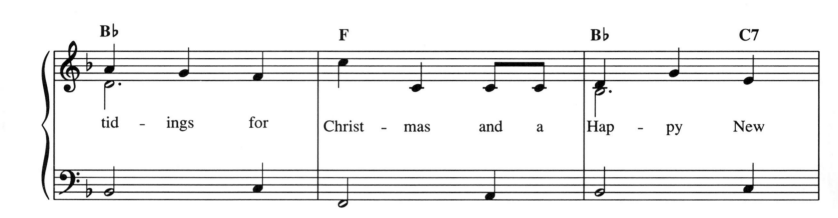

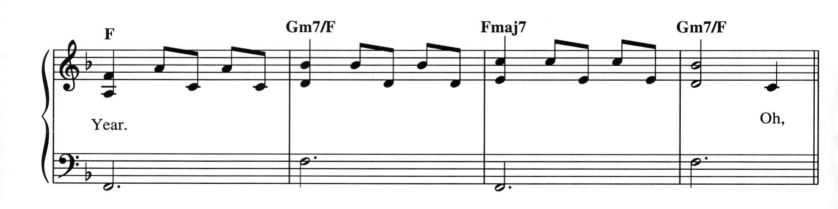

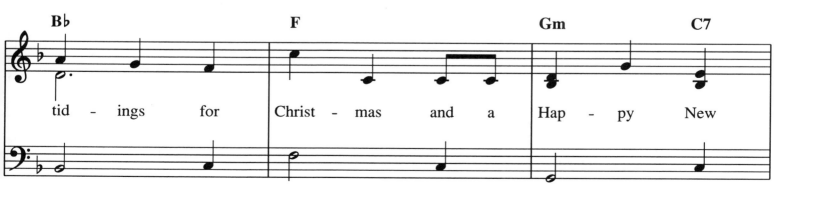

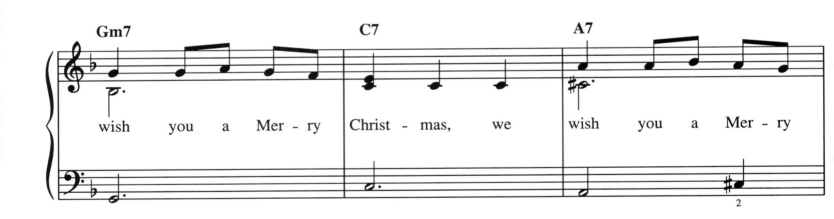

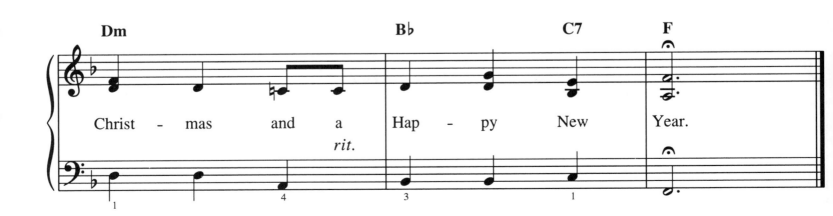

SANTA CLAUS IS COMIN' TO TOWN

Words by HAVEN GILLESPIE
Music by J. FRED COOTS

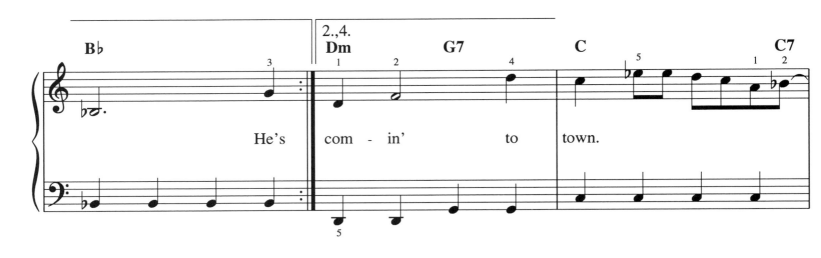

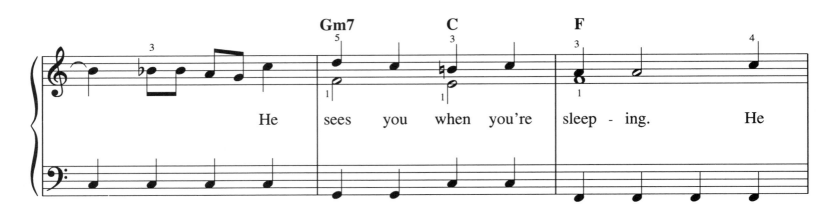

CODA

G   A7   D

sake!   Oh, you   bet - ter watch out,   you

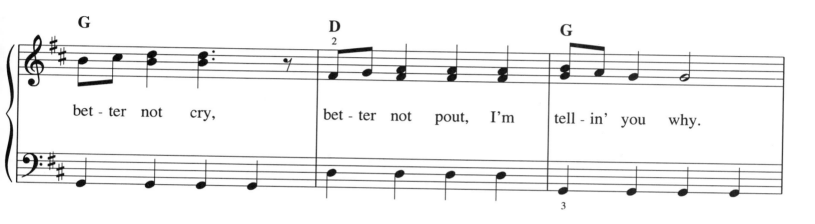

G   D   G

bet - ter not cry,   bet - ter not pout, I'm   tell - in' you why.

F#m   Bm   Em   A7   D   D7/C

San - ta Claus is   com - in'   to   town. ____

G/B   Gm/Bb   A7   N.C.   D

SNOW HO HO

Words and Music by
ROBIN FREDERICK

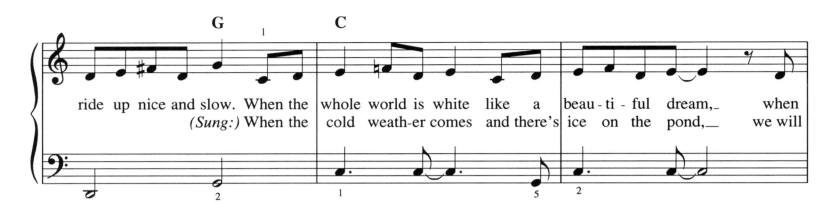

ride up nice and slow. When the | whole world is white like a | beau - ti - ful dream,_ when
(Sung:) When the | cold weath-er comes and there's | ice on the pond,_ we will

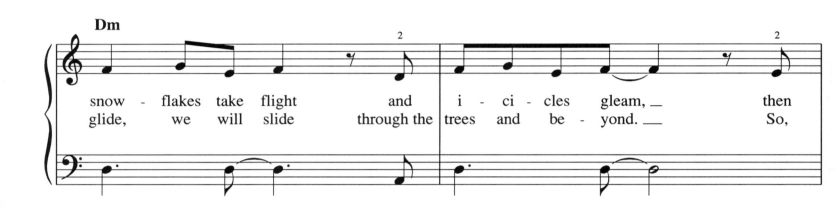

snow - flakes take flight and | i - ci - cles gleam, _ then
glide, we will slide through the | trees and be - yond. _ So,

come with me and a - | way we'll go in the | snow-ho - ho - ho - ho - ho - ho - ho -
take my hand and a - | way we'll go in the |

ho - ho - ho - ho - ho, in the | snow.

snow - ho - ho - ho - ho - ho - ho - ho - ho - ho - ho - ho - ho, in the

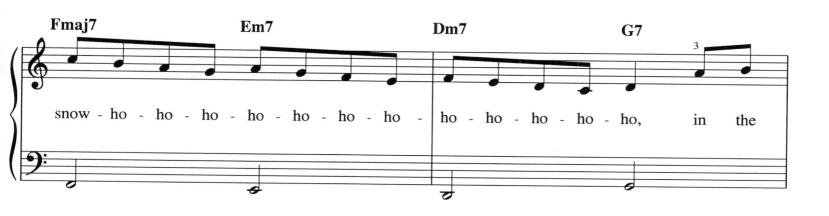

snow - ho - ho - ho - ho - ho - ho - ho - ho - ho - ho - ho - ho, in the

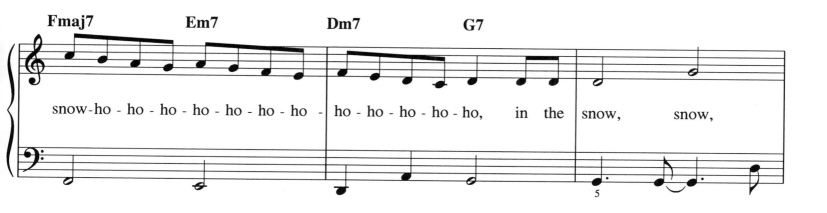

snow-ho - ho - ho - ho - ho - ho - ho - ho - ho - ho - ho - ho, in the snow, snow,

snow, snow, snow, in the snow!

DOWNTOWN HOLIDAY HULLABALOO

Words and Music by ROY ZIMMERMAN
and MELANIE HARBY

Moderately fast Jitterbug tempo

Folks in ev-'ry shop are bus-y look-ing for an op-por-tu-ni-
Here they come pa-rad-ing up and down the prom-e-nade and as they
Peo-ple on the bus-'ll start to jus-tle and to bus-tle 'cause they

hul - la - ba - loo, ___ it's a hul - la - ba - loo, ___ it's a

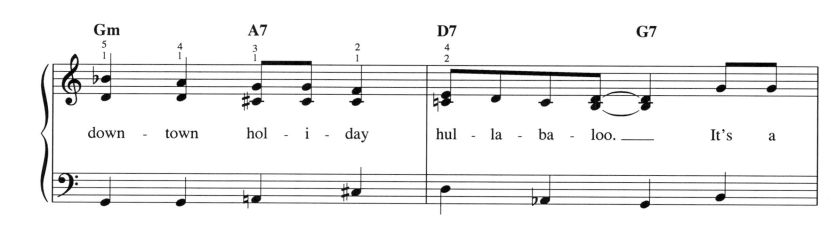

down - town hol - i - day hul - la - ba - loo. ___ It's a

hus - tle, bus - tle, hur - ly, bur - ly hub - bub, too. ___ It's a

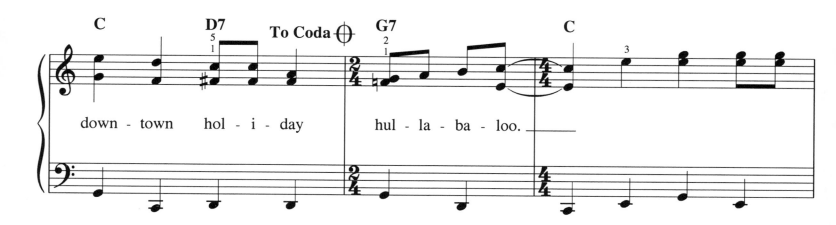

down - town hol - i - day hul - la - ba - loo.

D.S. al Coda

CODA

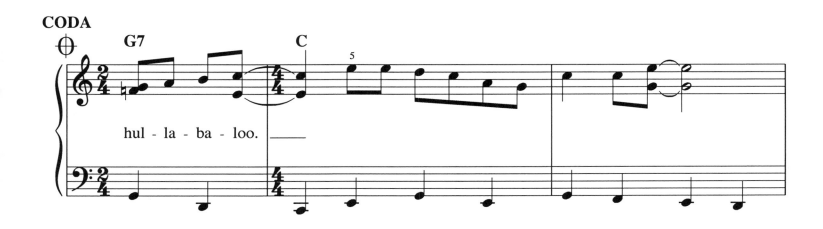

hul - la - ba - loo. _____

Friends are gon - na greet you,

yell - in' in the street "yoo - hoo,"

_____ *(Spoken:) a Merry Christmas to you! (Sung:)* It's a hul - la - ba - loo, _____ it's a

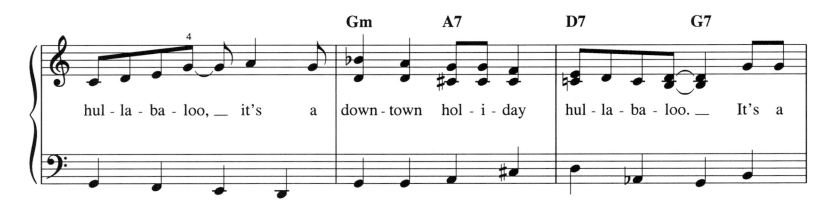

hul - la - ba - loo, __ it's a down - town hol - i - day hul - la - ba - loo. __ It's a

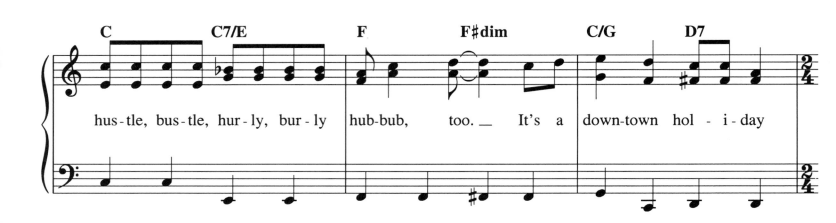

hus - tle, bus - tle, hur - ly, bur - ly hub - bub, too. __ It's a down - town hol - i - day

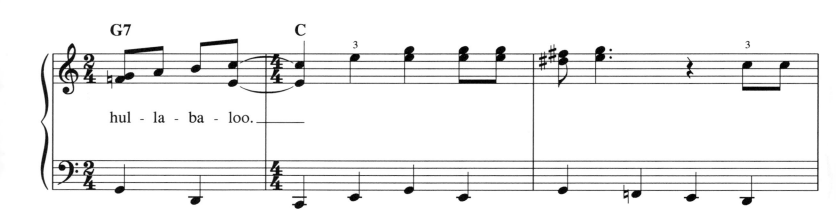

hul - la - ba - loo. __

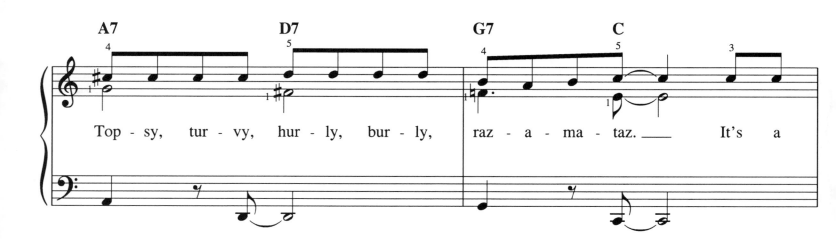

Top - sy, tur - vy, hur - ly, bur - ly, raz - a - ma - taz. __ It's a

hus - tle, bus - tle, hub - ble, bub - ble, all of that jazz. ___ It's a

raz - zle, daz - zle, ver - y Mer - ry Christ - mas to you. It's a

down - town hol - i - day hul - la - ba - loo. ___

I'D LIKE TO HAVE AN ELEPHANT FOR CHRISTMAS

Words and Music by
HANK THOMPSON

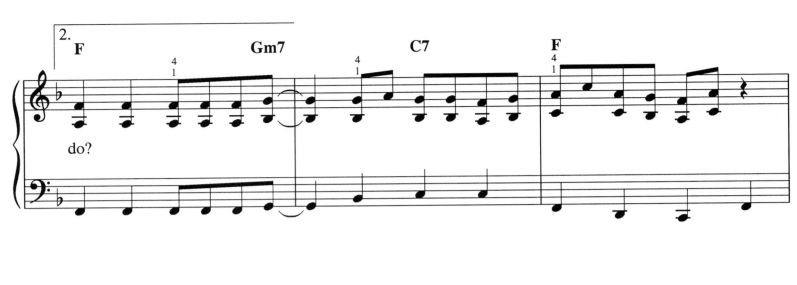

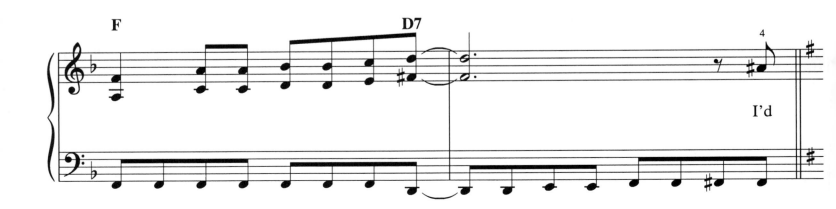

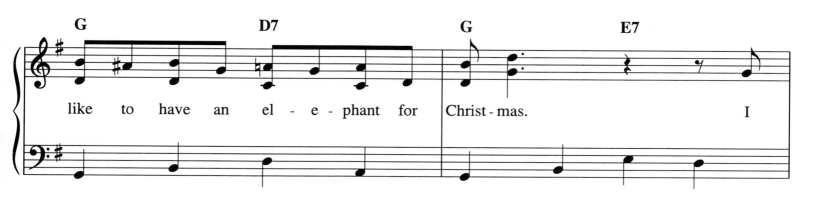

like to have an el - e - phant for Christ - mas. I

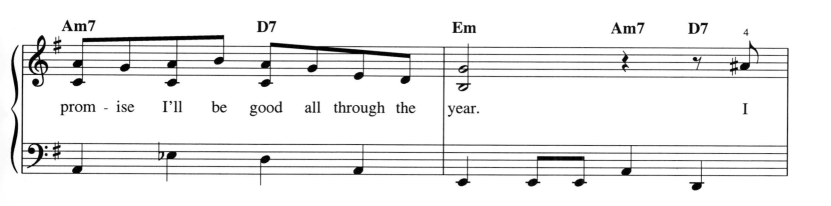

prom - ise I'll be good all through the year. I

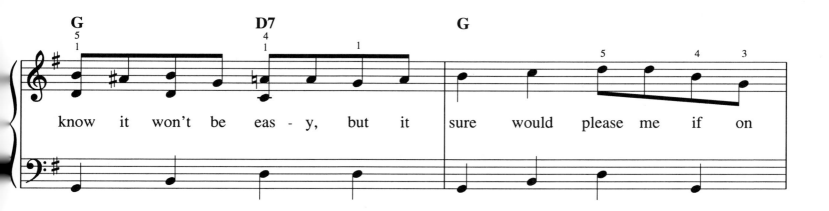

know it won't be eas - y, but it sure would please me if on

Christ-mas day my el - e-phant is here. I guess that I should ask for a

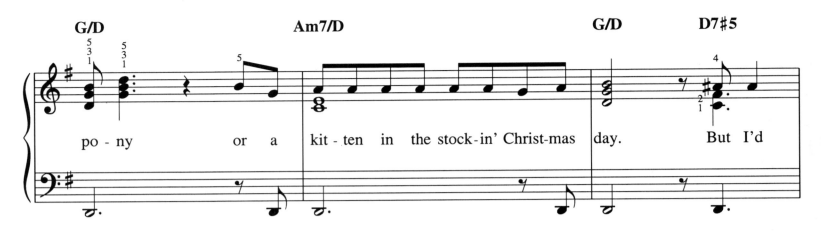

po - ny   or a   kit - ten in the stock-in' Christ-mas day.   But I'd

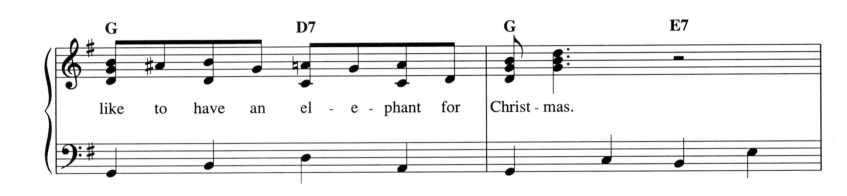

like to have an el - e -phant for   Christ - mas.

May - be, San - ta, you can find a   way.   I'd like to have an el - e-phant for

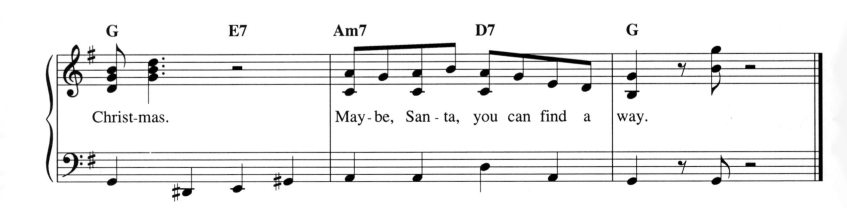

Christ-mas.   May - be, San - ta, you can find a   way.

AROUND THE WORLD CHRISTMAS

Words and Music by JIMMY HAMMER
and DAVE KINNOIN

Moderately, in one

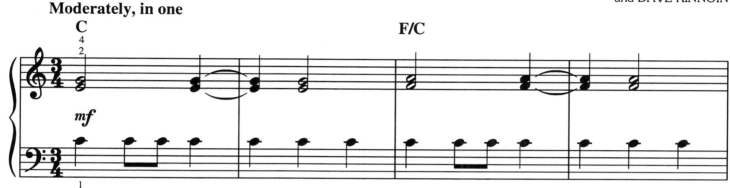

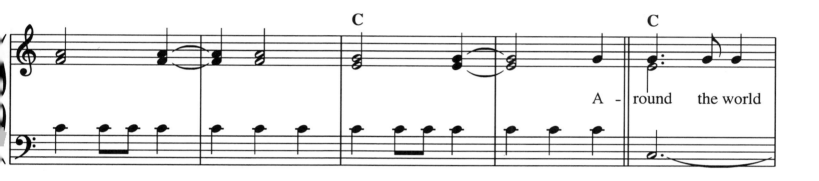

A - round   the world

Christ - mas   has   come   to   us   all;   with   won - der   and

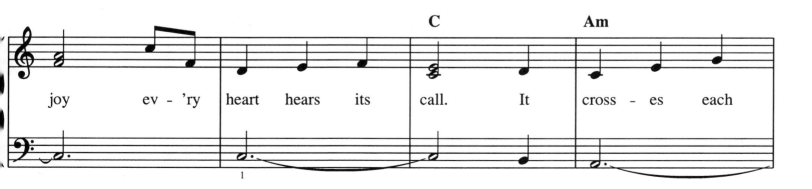

joy   ev - 'ry   heart   hears   its   call.   It   cross - es   each

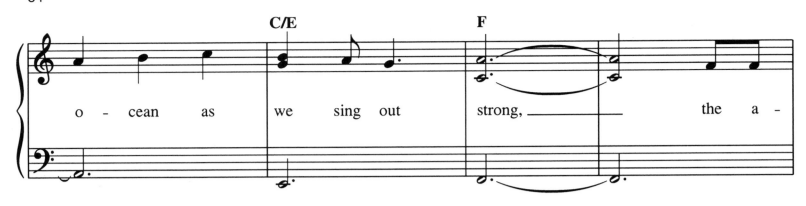

o - cean as we sing out strong, _____ the a -

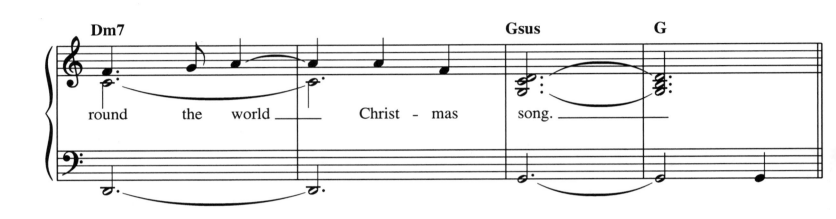

round the world _____ Christ - mas song. _____

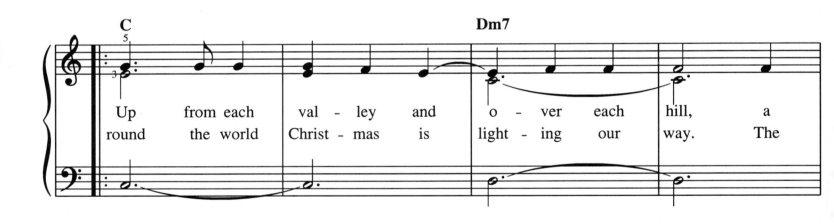

Up from each val - ley and o - ver each hill, a
round the world Christ - mas is light - ing our way. The

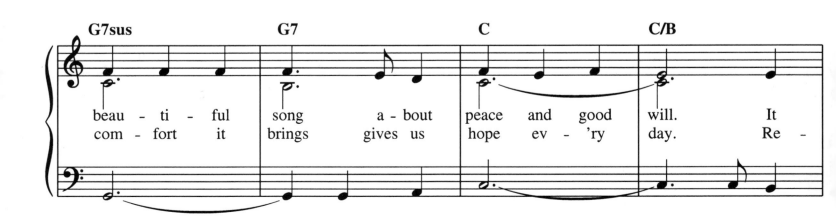

beau - ti - ful song a - bout peace and good will. It
com - fort it brings gives us hope ev - 'ry day. Re -

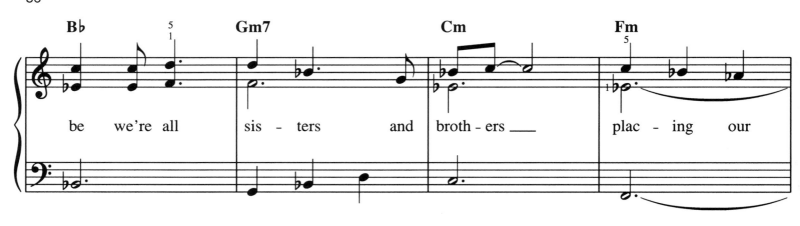

be   we're all   sis - ters   and   broth - ers ___   plac - ing   our

stars   on   the   same _____   Christ - mas   tree? _____   A -

same _____   Christ - mas   tree? _____   It   comes   to   all

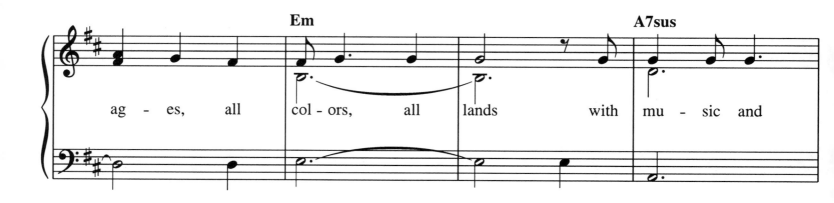

ag - es,   all   col - ors,   all   lands   with   mu - sic   and

57

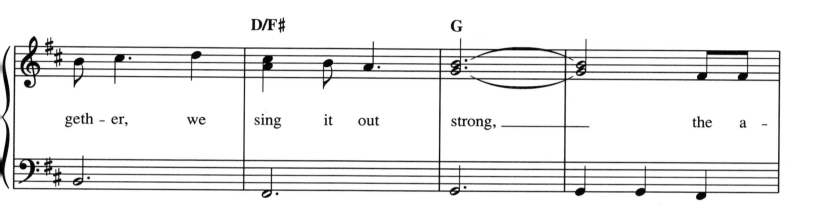

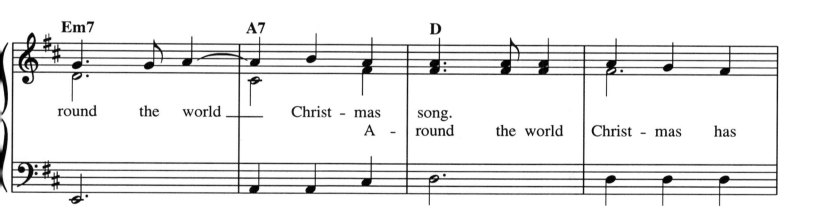

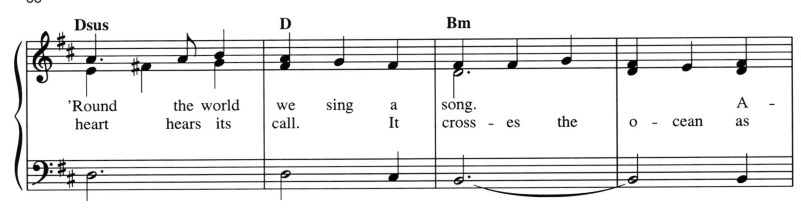

'Round the world we sing a song.
heart hears its call. It

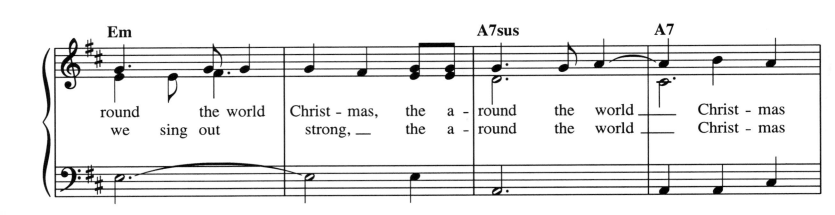

round the world Christ - mas, the a - round the world _____ Christ - mas
we sing out strong, _____ the a - round the world _____ Christ - mas

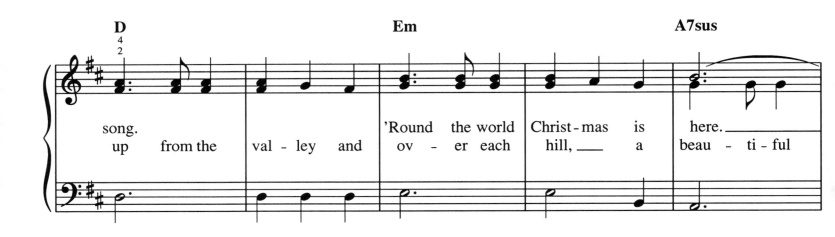

song. 'Round the world Christ - mas is here. _____
up from the val - ley and ov - er each hill, _____ a beau - ti - ful

_____ 'Round the world we sing a song.
song a - bout peace and good will. _____ It holds us to -

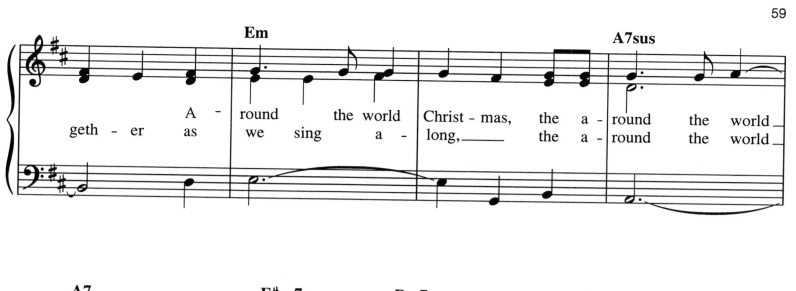

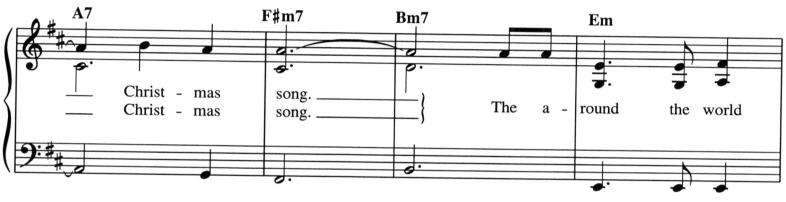

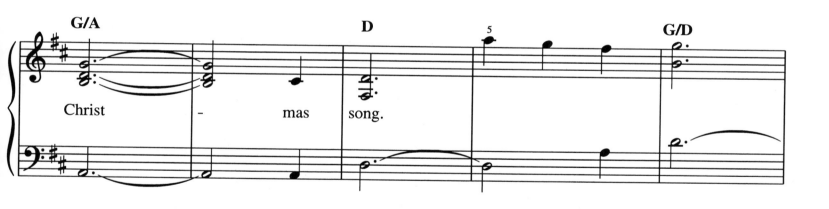

DECK THE HALLS

Traditional
Additional lyrics by ROBIN FREDERICK

Moderately

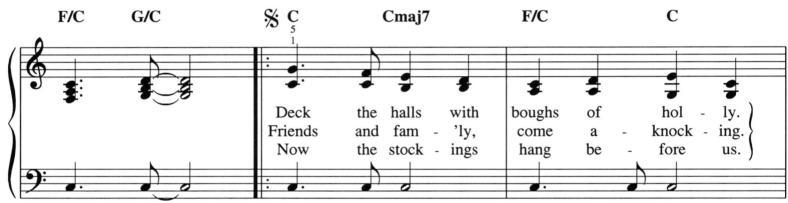

Deck the halls with boughs of hol - ly.
Friends and fam - 'ly, come a - knock - ing.
Now the stock - ings hang be - fore us.

Fa, la, la, la, la, la, la, la, la. To help us hang our
'Tis the sea - son Cel - e - brate them

to be jol - ly.
Christ - mas stock - ings.
with a cho - rus.

Fa, la, la, la, la, la, la, la, la.

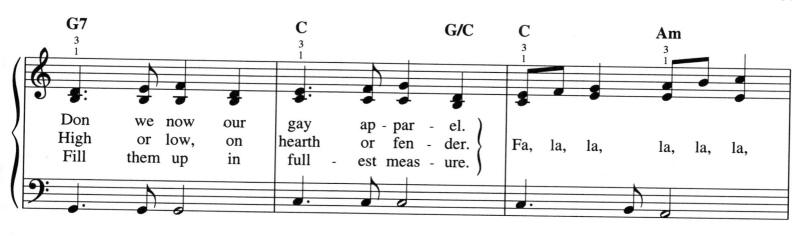

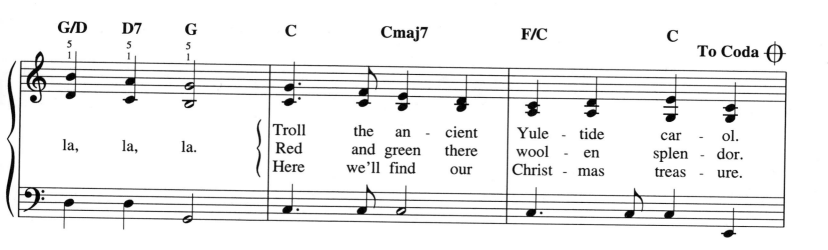

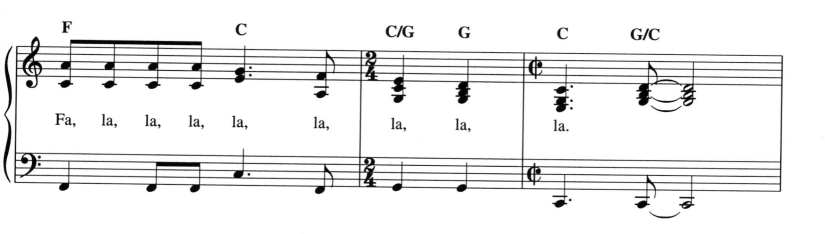

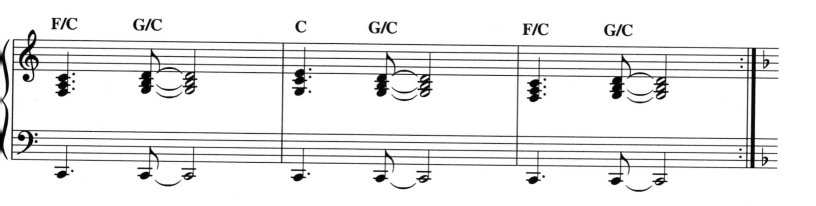

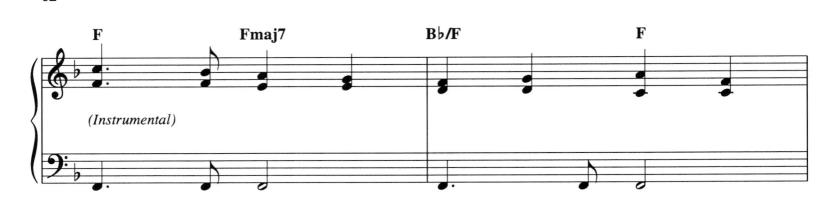

(Instrumental)

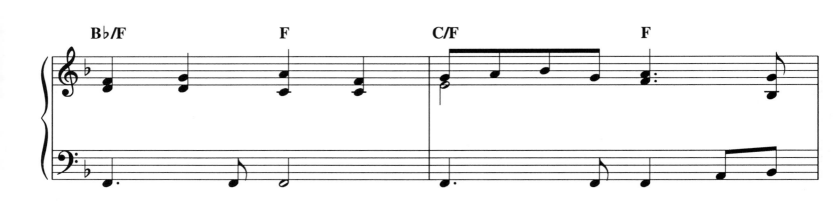

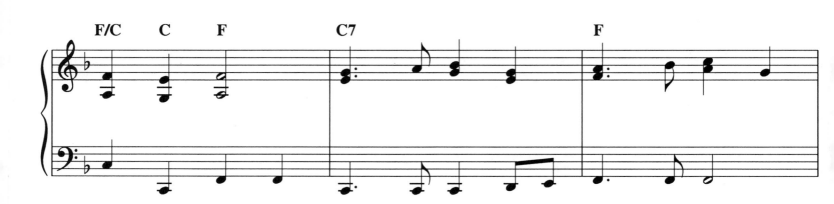

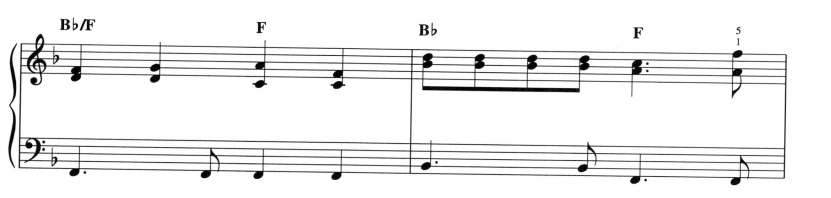

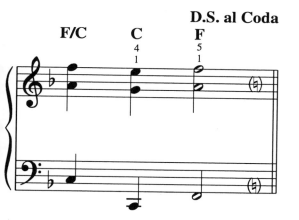

Fa, la, la, la, la, la,

la, la, la. Fa, la, la, la, la, la, la, la, la.

HE DELIVERS

Words and Music by
SANDY SHERMAN

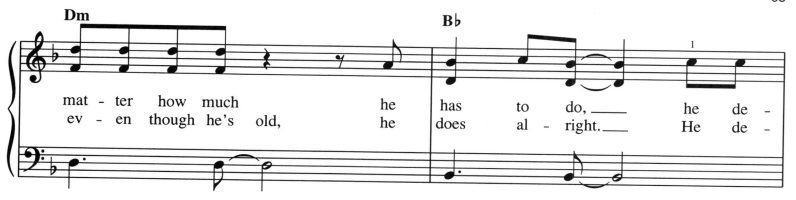

matter how much | he | has | to | do, | he de-
ev - en though he's old, | he | does | al - right. | He de-

liv-ers. He de-liv-ers, yeah, yeah, | he de-liv-ers. | In
liv-ers. He de-liv-ers, yeah, yeah, | he de-liv-ers. | So,

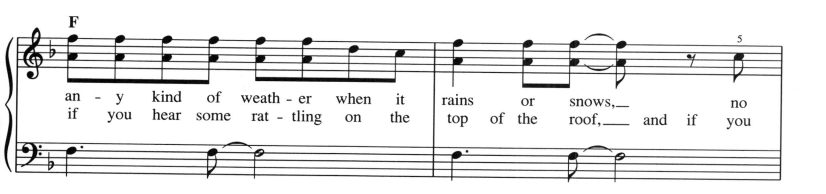

an - y kind of weath-er when it | rains or snows, | no
if you hear some rat-tling on the | top of the roof, and if you

mat-ter if there's i - ci - cles | on his nose, | with-
hear Plu-to bark-ing a | woof, woof, woof; if you

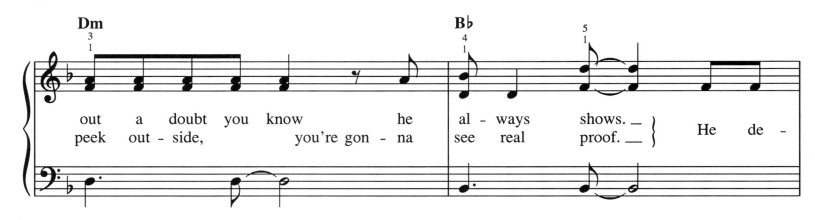

liv - ers in per - son just be - cause, ___ be -

cause he's the best, he's | 1. San - ta Claus. ___

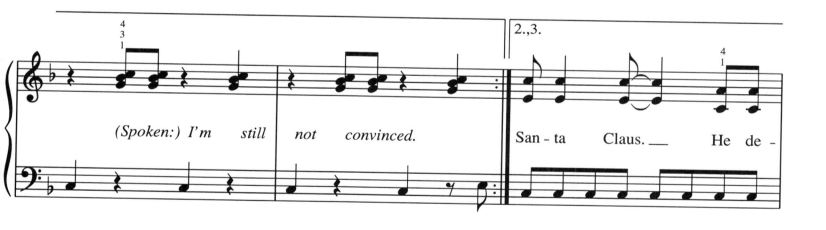

(Spoken:) I'm still not convinced. | 2.,3. San - ta Claus. ___ He de -

liv - ers ab - so - lute - ly free. ___

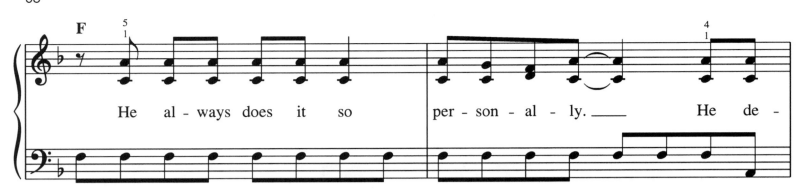

F

He al - ways does it so per - son - al - ly. _____ He de -

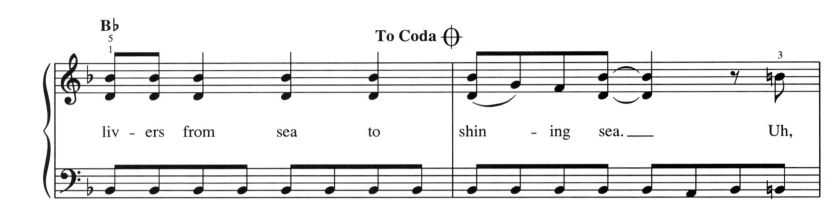

B♭

To Coda ⊕

liv - ers from sea to shin - ing sea. _____ Uh,

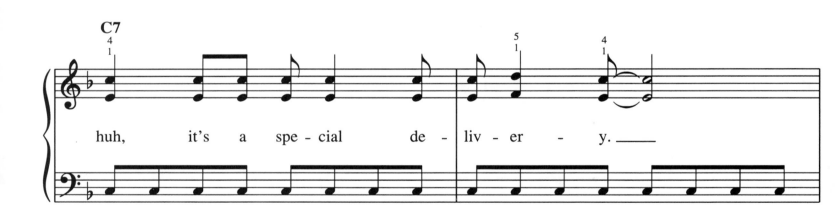

C7

huh, it's a spe - cial de - liv - er - y. _____

(Spoken:) It's not the florist or the *pizza man.* *He's not?* *He's not the plumber or a*

telegram. He isn't? It's not even the handy man. But, by

D.S. al Coda
(take 2nd ending)

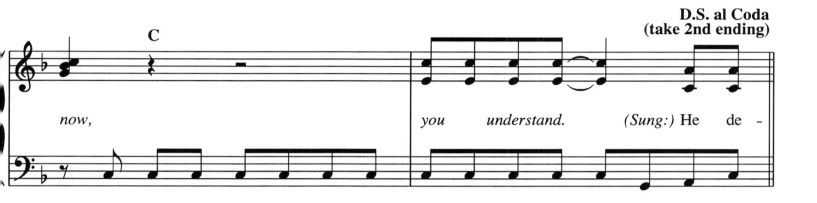

now, you understand. *(Sung:)* He de -

CODA

shin - ing sea.

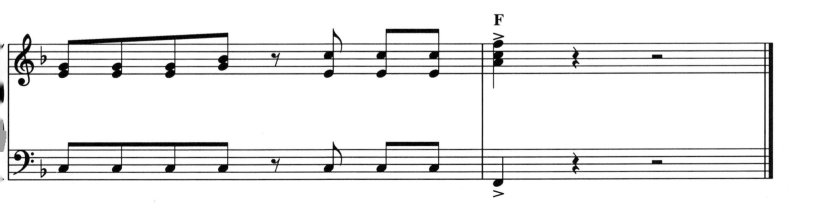

THE TWELVE DAYS OF CHRISTMAS
(REPRISE)

Traditional
New lyrics by ROBIN FREDERICK

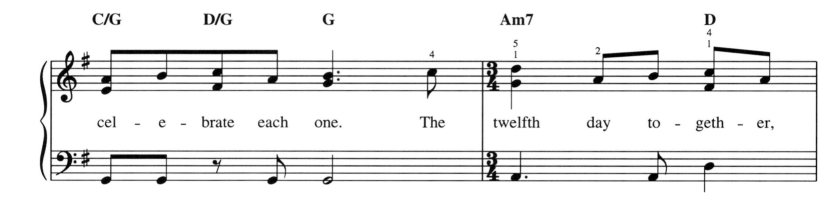

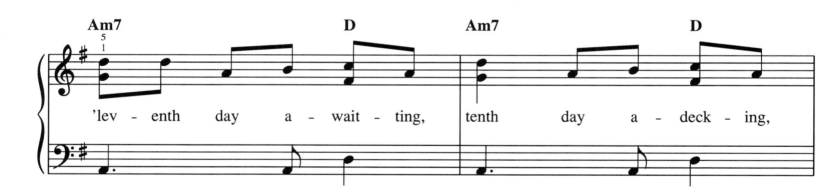

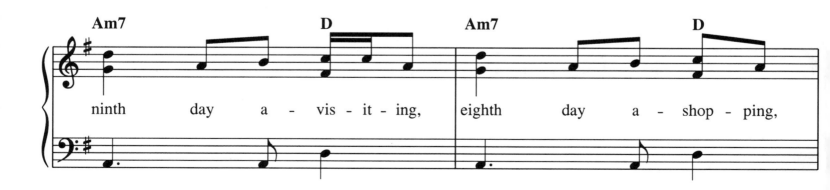